PRAYERS FOR EVERYDAY

Compiled by Elaine Sommers Rich

Elaine Sommers Rich
for Weldon and
Frances
Aug. 26, 1990

Faith and Life Press
Newton, Kansas

96   95   94   93   92   91   90   8   7   6   5   4   3   2   1

Library of Congress Number 90-80749
International Standard Book Number 0-87303-137-7

Editorial direction for Faith and Life Press by Maynard Shelly, general
editor; copyediting by Edna Dyck; design by John Hiebert. Printing by
Mennonite Press.

Foreword

I know Elaine Sommers Rich as a woman of prayer. It is no surprise to me that she has collected prayers over the years and decided to compile them for others to use. These prayers fit the contrasts and variety of our lives. Here are prayers for close at home and far away, the ordinary and the extraordinary. Some are long and eloquent; others are short and crisp and to the point. We can pray these prayers in solitude in our own private worship, in our small group, or in the midst of our congregation. These prayers will nourish our souls and enrich us on our faith journeys.

Prayer is a way to connect to God. We share our words with God. Listening is also involved. May we use quiet time to reflect, meditate, and listen as we offer these prayers to God.

In this prayer book, Elaine Sommers Rich helps us make connections. I know of another personal prayer book of Elaine's. It is the birthday book that she carries with her, collecting signatures from new friends. As I was signing my name on my birthday page in her book, I was surprised to learn that an acquaintance from another city shared my day. A friendship has deepened because of this connection. We pray for each other throughout the year and especially on our birthday. We both know that Elaine is also praying for us on that day.

May our connections with God and with each other have deeper meaning as a result of these prayers.

NORMA J. JOHNSON

Executive Secretary
Commission on Education
General Conference Mennonite Church

Contents

With joyful thanks to sleep
No darkness me molest
Soften to us our enemies
Give your angels charge
Brightness be about our beds
Evening prayers for children
  Love takes care of us
  In safety sleep
  Beauty everywhere
  Arms of love
  Tender shepherd
  While my heart is tender

Fruits of the earth
Table spread
Sustain us
Bless this meal
Be our guest
All eyes look to you
To work and serve
Fresh tokens of love
Receive true bread
Black mother's prayer
Being loved and wanted
Table prayers for children
  Be present at our table
  All good gifts
  Bread on every table

Sunday morning
Another prayer for Sunday
Sunday evening
Advancing years
Family reunion

Family finances
Outlook the mark of time
Childbirth
Parents for their children
Mother for her daughter
After a quarrel
Understanding another
For missionaries
Thanksgiving for trees
Christmas kin
Work for the new year
Special times for children
  New year
  New baby
  First day at school
  Birthday

Open our eyes of faith
Grow from glory to glory
Find the center of our lives
When not in joy or stress
In the dryness of August
Transformed for witness
Lay our burdens in God's hands
From students in Botswana
New year mercies
True hosannas
Easter overcomes
Going back to school
College discipleship
Thanksgiving
Late autumn
Night before Christmas
Born on Christmas
Baptized into a family

The Lord's Prayer

The Lord's Prayer is really the disciples' prayer.

Our Father in heaven,
hallowed be your name
Your kingdom come
Your will be done,
  on earth as it is in heaven
Give us this day our daily bread
And forgive us our debts,
  as we also forgive our debtors
And do not bring us to the time of trial,
  but rescue us from the evil one.
Matthew 6:9-13

Other ancient manuscripts add this doxology: For the kingdom and the power and the glory are yours forever. Amen.

Prayer of Francis of Assisi

The following beloved prayer is ascribed to Francis of Assisi (1181-1226), Italy.

Lord, make me an instrument of your peace.
Where there is hatred, let me sow love,
Where there is injury, pardon,
Where there is doubt, faith,
Where there is despair, hope,
Where there is darkness, light,
Where there is sadness, joy.

O Divine Master, grant that I may
not so much seek to be consoled as to console,
not so much to be understood as to understand,
not so much to be loved, as to love;
for it is in giving that we receive,
it is in pardoning that we are pardoned,
it is in dying that we are born to eternal life.
Amen

Morning

O Lord, in the morning you hear my voice;
   in the morning I plead my case to you, and
      watch. Psalm 5:3

Very early in the morning, while it was still
dark, Jesus got up, left the house and went off
to a solitary place, where he prayed.
Mark 1:35 (New International Version)

New day for a purpose

The following two prayers are from the old Amish devotional book *Ernsthafte Christenpflicht*, dating back to 1739 or earlier. Pathway Publishing Corporation published it in English in 1967 as *A Devoted Christians's Prayer Book*.

Dear God, loving heavenly Father, you are our creator and provider, under whose loving care we have enjoyed another night of rest. We praise and thank you for this rest and for the new day. We ask you, O Father, to forgive us wherein we have misused any of your great blessings. We repent of all that we have done against your will.

Help us to remember that you have given us this new day for a purpose, to use wisely in holiness and godliness. May your holy name be honored and praised, and our souls be kept by grace unto eternal salvation. May your Holy Spirit lead us, and your guardian angels guide us on our way. O God, we ask this in the name of your beloved son, Jesus Christ, who taught us to pray, Our Father . . .

Be on guard this day

Dear loving Father, we bow before you this morning to thank you for another night's rest, for watching over us and keeping us from all harm. We thank you for the dawn of a new day, for the opportunities and privileges it brings. We pray that you guide and direct our lives today in the use of these benefits to your honor and glory.

We confess that we are unworthy of so many blessings. So often we forget the ways in which you have helped us. We become impatient and complain when we cannot have our own way. Forgive us these many faults and sins against you. Help us, O Lord, to do better today, and to be more grateful. It is only by your boundless mercy that our lives have been spared. Judge us not according to our deeds, but grant us mercy through the blood of Jesus Christ, who gave his life for us.

O heavenly Father, let us be on our guard this day against unclean and lustful thoughts. Keep us from self-righteousness and pride, and from any evil that may secretly enter our hearts. Cleanse us from any fault we do not see. Let our thoughts, our words and deeds, ever be pure, kind, and good. Show us the good in others, that we may love our neighbors as ourselves. May we be eager to bear each other's burdens in Christian love.

We pray, O Lord, for all our fellow Christians, wherever they may be. Especially do we pray for the ministers and teachers who are laboring to make known your word and your will in many parts of the earth. Supply their every need, comfort and strengthen them, and protect them from every danger. Give them wisdom and discernment to perform their duties in a way that is pleasing to you. Cause us to remember those who labor in your vineyard, and to assist them in anything they need.

We pray for all those who are still living in sin, who do not yet know you. May they repent and obtain salvation in this time of grace. O Lord, we pray for those who are new in the faith. Help them to grow, and keep them firmly anchored on Jesus Christ the rock of their salvation. Keep them from falling, and help them to live a victorious life, a true testimony for you.

We pray for those who have strayed from the narrow way and have fallen again into sin. O that they might see how grievously they have erred and repent and again find peace for their souls. We pray, O heavenly Father, for those who have authority over us, for the rulers and governments of every nation. Lead them according to your holy will. Make us worthy of a government which allows us the freedom to serve them.

O Lord, we pray for those who are sick, in sorrow or pain,

for those who are discouraged. We pray for the widows and the fatherless, for the aged and afflicted, and for those who suffer for your name's sake.

Into your hands we commit ourselves, our children, parents, brothers and sisters, friends, and all who are dear to us. Protect us this day against all dangers, both to body and soul. Give us a home where love, peace, and joy abound. Help us to be patient, kind, and good to one another. May your Holy Spirit lead us and the holy angels attend our way. Teach us to pray in spirit and truth, even as your son Jesus Christ has taught us, Our Father . . .

Until shadows lengthen

John Henry Newman (1801-1890), leader of the Oxford Movement in England, often used the following prayer. Whether he actually wrote it is uncertain.

O Lord, support us all the day long, until the shadows lengthen and the evening comes, and the busy world is hushed, and the fever of life is over, and our work is done. Then, Lord, in your mercy grant us a safe lodging and a holy rest, and peace at last; through Jesus Christ our Lord. Amen.

Another chance

This poem appeared in the January 16, 1968, *Gospel Herald*. Barbara Esch Shisler (b. 1937), Telford, Pennsylvania, is a freelance writer and the mother of three grown children.

Thank you, Lord,
for a new opportunity, another chance,
this fresh day, clean and untarnished.
I abused yesterday, violated the day
with petty fussings and shallow purposes,
creating tumults over trifles,
self-centeredly aware of my own feelings
at the expense of others.
Thank you for this innocent day.
Let me live every moment in you,
for each moment is a new day,
another chance.

Our work is useful work

Walter Rauschenbusch (1861-1918) believed that the teachings of Jesus should apply to all areas of life. *For God and the People, Prayers of the Social Awakening*, was published by Pilgrim Press in 1910. In its introduction, he said, "We need to blaze new paths to God for the feet of modern men."

O God, we thank you for the sweet refreshment of sleep and for the glory and vigor of the new day. As we set our faces once more toward our daily work, we pray you for the strength sufficient for our tasks. May Christ's spirit of duty and service ennoble all we do. Uphold us by the consciousness that our work is useful work and a blessing to all. If there has been anything in our work harmful to others and dishonorable to ourselves, reveal it to our inner eye with such clearness that we shall hate it and put it away, though it be at a loss to ourselves. When we work with others, help us to regard them not as servants to our will, but as brothers and sisters, equal to us in human dignity, and equally worthy of their full reward. May there be nothing in this day's work of which we shall be ashamed when the sun has set, nor in the eventide of our life when our task is done and we go to our long home to meet you face to face. Amen.

Snowflake prayer

Grace Whitehead, Kokomo, Indiana, is fond of "The Snowflake Prayer." Why is it called that? Charles Francis Whiston, who wrote the prayer, says: "What a single prayer can accomplish is exceedingly small, immeasurably small, and as insignificant as a single snowflake. But over the years, the faithful praying of this snowflake prayer will accumulate into a mighty snow pack, and it will slowly and thoroughly grind away the granite-like mass of self-sovereignty in us." The prayer is from *When Ye Pray Say Our Father* (Pilgrim Press, 1960), p. 455.

O holy God, in obedience to your claim, I surrender myself to you this day, all that I am and all that I have, to become wholly and unconditionally yours for your using. Take me from myself, and use me up as you will, where you will, when you will, with whom you will. Amen.

You let this new day dawn

An old Mennonite prayer book known as *Äpfel in Silberne Schalen (Golden Apples in Silver Bowls)* was published in Switzerland in 1702 and reprinted at the Ephrata Cloister, Pennsylvania, in 1742. Elizabeth Horsch Bender did this translation for the Historical Committee of the Mennonite Church.

Lord God, dear heavenly Father,
  our Creator and Provider,
  under whose gracious protection and care
    we rested well last night,
  for this we praise and thank you.
Whatever misuse we may meanwhile have made,
  dear Father, of your benevolence,
  whatever has been in any way contrary
    to your divine will,
  we penitently confess.

Forgive us for the sake of your dear son Jesus.
Teach us to reflect on why you have let
  this new day dawn,
  so that we may spend it,
    and all the coming days of our lives,
  soberly, righteously, and devoutly,
  that your holy name may be honored
        and praised,
  and that we may be graciously kept
        and eternally saved.
May your Holy Spirit guide us,
  and may your good angels make our path happy.
This we pray in the name of your beloved Son,
      Jesus Christ,
  who taught us to pray, "Our Father . . ."

Do some work of peace

South African writer Alan Paton (1905-1988) wrote this as he meditated on the great prayer of Saint Francis of Assisi. It was published in his book *Instrument of Thy Peace*, Copyright © 1982 by Seabury Press. Reprinted by permission of Harper & Row, Publishers, Inc.

Help me, O Lord, to be more loving. Help me, O Lord, not to be afraid to love the outcast, the leper, the unmarried pregnant woman, the traitor to the State, the man out of prison. Help me by my love to restore the faith of the disillusioned, the disappointed, the early bereaved. Help me by my love to be the witness of your love.

And may I this coming day be able to do some work of peace for you.

Right in the right spirit

This handwritten prayer was found in the posthumous papers of Pauline Krehbiel Raid (1907-1984), Bluffton, Ohio.

Help me, O God, to meet in the right way and in the right spirit everything which comes to me today. Help me to approach my work cheerfully and my tasks diligently.

Help me to meet disappointments, frustrations, hindrances, opposition calmly and without irritation. Help me to meet delays with patience and unreasonable demands with self-control.

Help me to accept praise modestly and criticism without losing my temper.

Keep me serene all through today.

If I know there are things which annoy the people with whom I live and work, help me not to do them. If I know there are things which would please them, help me to go out of my way to do them. Equip me today, O God, with the constant awareness of your presence, which will make me do everything as unto you. Grant that others may see in me something of the reflection of the Master whose I am and whom I seek to serve. This I ask for your love's sake. Amen.

Prayers for children

We used the following prayers with our children when they were young. Sources of the first two prayers are unknown. The third was written by Paul Adams, Bluffton, Ohio, a Lutheran minister. The fourth has been attributed to Rebecca J. Weston (born c. 1890).

Father, bless your child today,
Make me good and kind, I pray.
Amen.

Jesus, friend of little children,
  Close beside me all the day,
Help me to be kind and thoughtful
  In my work and in my play.
Amen.

For this new morning and its light,
For rest and shelter of the night,
For health and food, for love and friends,
For everything your goodness sends,
Father in heaven, we thank you.
Amen.

Father, we thank you for the night,
And for the pleasant morning light;
For rest and food and loving care,
And all that makes the day so fair.

Help us to do the things we should,
To be to others kind and good;
In all we do, at work or play,
To love you better day by day.
Amen.

Noon

Clock hands now point straight up.
Everywhere people pause for lunch hour, a
change of pace, refreshment for the body. May
it also be a time for refreshment of spirit.

Evening and morning and at noon
  I utter my complaint and moan,
  and he will hear my voice. Psalm 55:17

In whom we live

Simon Patrick (1626-1707) was a minister in the Church of England.

Almighty and most merciful Father, in whom we live and move and have our being, to whose tender compassion we owe our safety in days past, together with all the comforts of this present life, and the hopes of that which is to come; we praise you, O God, our Creator. Unto you we give thanks, O God, our exceeding joy. You daily pour your benefits upon us. Grant, we ask you, that Jesus our Lord, the hope of glory, may be formed in us, in all humility, meekness, patience, contentedness, and absolute surrender of our souls and bodies to your holy will and pleasure. Leave us not, nor forsake us, O Father, but conduct us safe through all changes of our condition here, in an unchangeable love to you, and in holy tranquility of mind in your love to us, till we come to dwell with you, and rejoice in you forever. Amen.

On unknown ways

Aron P. Toews (1887-?1938), a Mennonite minister in Russia, kept a diary while he was exiled to hard labor in Siberia. In 1936 as, far away from his family, he contemplated the coming Christmas and New Year season, he wrote the following lines. They are taken from *Siberian Diary of Aron P. Toews,* with a biography by Olga Rempel, translated by Esther Klaassen Bergen (CMBC Publications, Winnipeg, 1984), p. 121.

Lord Jesus, lead us day by day
On unknown ways, yet blessedly.
Amen.

No improper feeling

Elizabeth Fry (1780-1845), an English Quaker, pioneered in securing better care for prisoners.

O Lord, may I be directed what to do and what to leave undone and then may I humbly trust that a blessing will be with me in my various engagements.

Enable me, O Lord, to feel tenderly and charitably toward all my beloved fellow mortals. Help me to have no soreness or improper feelings toward any. Let me think no evil, bear all things, hope all things, endure all things.

Let me walk in all humility and godly fear before all people and in your sight. Amen.

Fragrance everywhere

Mother Teresa of India cherishes this prayer by John Henry Newman. See the note on page 7.

Help me to spread your fragrance everywhere I go—let me preach you without preaching, not by words but by my example—by the catching force, the sympathetic influence of what I do, the evident fullness of the love my heart bears to you. Amen.

Your love prepares

The following two prayers are favorites of Royal and Evelyn Bauer, Goshen, Indiana. The first is by John M. Drescher (b. 1928), a Mennonite writer, who formerly edited the *Gospel Herald*.

O God,
I cannot fathom
your love for me,
but as I thank you
that it is everlasting,
I can only confess
that the source of my love
for you
is your love for me,
and that, when I wander,
your love
always prepares the way
for my sad return
in repentance.
Forgive my wandering ways
and lead me
to that larger love
shown in your
giving all for me.
Amen.

Give me freedom

Robert Raines (b. 1926) is a Methodist bishop. This prayer appears in his book *Creative Brooding*, ©1966 Robert Raines. Reprinted with permission of Macmillan Publishing Company, p. 101.

I love this life!
I want to live it to the full.
Don't let me miss anything good,
nor scorn those who find what I have missed.

Lord, give me freedom
to rejoice in your gifts of life and love,
to be present in all that I do,
and to praise you with all my strength.
Amen.

During the day for children

Here is a sheaf of noon or during-the-day prayers for children. The first is by Bertha C. Krall, the second by a nine-year-old boy; sources for the other three are unknown.

For your many gifts we thank you;
for the gift of seeing things and people;
for the gift of hearing loud and soft sounds;
for the gift of tasting food and drink;
for the gift of feeling things we touch;
for the gift of smelling the scent of flowers—
for your many gifts, we thank you.
Amen.

Dear God, please help us to remember you when we are in trouble. Help us also to remember you when we are happy. Help us to do right. We thank you for our parents, homes, schools, and most of all for the Bible and Jesus. Amen.

Lord, teach us to love your children everywhere, because you are their father and mother and mine. Amen.

Lord, bless my playmates, this I pray.
Bless us together while we play.
Bless us apart, and make us know
Your love wherever we may go.
Amen.

Dear Jesus, help us make our home
A place where you would love to stay,
Where there is happiness and joy,
And cheerfulness the livelong day.
May father, mother, sister, brother
Be bound by cords of love,
Till home on earth shall be just like
A bit of home above.
Amen.

Evening

He went up the mountain by himself to pray.
When evening came, he was there alone.

Matthew 14:23

Angels attend us

This evening prayer is from the Amish prayer book *Ernsthafte Christenpflicht*. See note on page 4.

O Lord God, kind and merciful Father, this day you again so graciously shed abroad the light of heaven upon our pathway and gave us another opportunity to serve you and to grow in godliness.

For these many blessings we are grateful to you, O heavenly Father, and would praise and glorify your name forever. Forgive us, Lord, where we have sinned against you, for we confess with sorrow and regret that we have often through carelessness and neglect transgressed your law. Forgive us for the sake of your dear son, Jesus Christ, in whose name we pray. Receive and pardon us in his name that we may be reconciled to you and abide eternally in your peace.

We pray you, O heavenly Father, keep us this night and for the rest of our lives under the shadow and protection of your wings. Shield us from the power of the evil one who is continually trying to deceive us and to destroy our souls.

Grant us a peaceful night's rest according to your will. Refresh our bodies, minds, and spirits, so that we may be found watching and waiting, eagerly looking forward to the glorious reappearing of your beloved son when he comes to claim his own.

O holy and merciful Father, let the light of your loving kindness illuminate our pathway, lest the gloom of darkness that engulfs the world should also envelop us and lull us to a spiritual death. Rather, let us arise and walk in newness of life, all to the honor and glory of your holy name, and to our eternal salvation.

We pray, O loving Father, for all your children who are in need. Especially do we remember the sick and weak, the sorrowing and troubled, and those who suffer for your name's sake. We also pray for our enemies and for those who mistreat us, for they do not realize what they are doing.

We pray that you would send faithful workers into your harvest and ministers who preach your holy word according to your will. We pray for the government of our land, and for the heads of all nations and cities, also for all sorrowful oppressed and destitute souls.

You know all our needs, dear Father. We pray that you will give each one of us what is of greatest service to us. Protect us with your great power and watch over us, for we are your creation, the work of your hands. Prepare us for your eternal salvation. All this we pray in the name of your dear son, Jesus Christ, who has taught us to ask in his name, Our Father. . . .

We commit ourselves, dear Father, with all our loved ones into your hands. May your angels attend us this night and your Holy Spirit guide us through the tribulations of this life. Help us to face death with confidence, and to arise with joy to enter our eternal home. This we ask in the name of your beloved son Jesus Christ. Amen.

My guiding sun

In 1925, Aron P. Toews (page 14), living in Rosental, a Mennonite village in the Ukraine, enclosed the following prayer by "the godly poet Immanuel Geibel" in a letter to his friend and parishioner Nikolai Kroeker, Chortitza.

O Lord, who in my heart abides,
Through joys and sorrows safely guides,
Be ever near.

Through summer's scorching heat and burdened toil,
In rosy spring of youth where pleasures smile,
Be ever near.

Keep me from wantonness and pride,
When I despair, be at my side,
And very near.

Your gracious blessing falls as morning dew.
Though helpless, I would dare the best for you.
Be ever near.

My comforter, my strength, my guiding sun,
O Lord, at journey's end, when day is done,
Be ever near.
Amen.

As those who hold your hand

Christoph Blumhardt (1843-1919) took over his father Johann's pastoral work at his death in 1880 at Bad Boll, near Stuttgart, Germany. A community of about fifty people lived and worked there together. We can be grateful to the Hutterian Brethren, *Lift Thine Eyes, Evening Prayers*, Ulster Park, New York, for making available the Blumhardt prayers in English. Their small volume contains an evening prayer for every day of the year. This prayer and the four that follow it are by Christoph Blumhardt.

Lord, our God, we thank you because you have helped us, and you help us again and again so that we can stand before you and be glad in our hearts in the complete certainty and faith that you are guiding and leading our lives and that we may look forward to a goal that will be revealed to all people. Protect us when in the silence we seem to be lonely; and keep us firm and strong in temptation and in the confusions of life so that we may stay bright and clear, as those who walk holding your hand and who are permitted to stand high above everything that is transitory. Amen.

What you have promised must come

Dear Father in heaven, we trust in your words, in the Word of life, of the eternal life given to us in Jesus Christ our Savior. We build on this in these days when so much is becoming weak and poor, and yet there is so much longing in people's hearts. And you will not let our hope come to nothing, for what you have promised must come, and what is promised in Jesus Christ must come to be, not only for a few but for the whole world, for which he died and was awakened from the dead. Be with us then, and grant that we may always be so alive that our life is radiant because of all the good that we are allowed to experience, and so that we become conquerors of all the evil which tries to attack us. We thank you for calling us again and again to life and giving us something new again and again. Praised be your name forever among us! Amen.

Strong in all paths of life

Lord our God, we thank you for all you do and have done for us, for the deliverance from need and death, and for all the signs that you hear us when we set our hopes in you, when we do not despair or become weak in anything so that even sin and death cannot frighten us; for you stand by us in everything and are not hindered by our imperfections from giving us more and more blessings. May the light in our hearts never be extinguished, the light that enables us to look into heaven and earth and perceive the good that comes our way today. Grant that we may remain glad and be a community that is strong in all paths of life to your praise and honor. Amen.

Strong in patient waiting

Lord our God, we thank you that you have given us a wonderful future as a foundation on which we can live, in which we can forget our present affliction and can believe that today goodness can already touch us, opposing death and opposing sin and opposing everything evil. Grant that we may become lighthearted and remain strong in patient waiting for the great day which is to come. And let today's history help toward the solution of all problems. We praise your name, our Father in the heavens! We praise you, for you are already good to us today and will yet bring clarity to everything on earth to the glory of your name. Amen.

Sleep with joyful thanks

Dear Father in heaven, how lovingly you have thought of us! How much good you have already given us and you allow us to experience again and again! So our hearts are joyful, truly joyful, and with joyful thanks we want to go to sleep, with joy in our hearts as your children. This shall be our service to you day and night. More than this you do not ask; but in this we will be faithful. We will be joyful; with joy we will look ahead in our life. And even if dark things come our way, yet we have the hope that your salvation is coming! Lord our God, we rejoice in this for the future as well as in the present. We rejoice in what you already give us today. Amen.

No darkness me molest

Thomas Ken (1637-1711), a royal chaplain to King Charles II of
England, was deprived of his bishopric for refusal to take the
oath to William and Mary. He is the author of the words of the
beloved Hymn 606 in the *Mennonite Hymnal*. The last stanza of
this poem, sometimes sung to Tallis' Canon, is on page 496 of the
Mennonite Hymnal.

All praise to thee, my God, this night,
For all the blessings of the light.
Keep me, O keep me, King of kings,
Beneath thine own almighty wings.

Forgive me, Lord, for thy dear Son,
The ill that I this day have done;
That with the world, myself, and thee,
I, ere I sleep, at peace may be.

O may my soul on thee repose,
And with sweet sleep my eyelids close,
Sleep that shall me more vig'rous make
To serve my God when I awake.

When in the night I sleepless lie,
My soul with heav'nly thoughts supply!
Let no ill dreams disturb my rest,
No powers of darkness me molest!

Praise God, from whom all blessings flow;
Praise him, all creatures here below;
Praise him above, ye heav'nly host:
Praise Father, Son, and Holy Ghost.
Amen.

Soften to us our enemies

Robert Louis Stevenson (1850-1894) wrote this family prayer for his household in Samoa.

Lord, behold our family here assembled. We thank you for this place in which we dwell, for the love that unites us, for the peace accorded us this day, for the hope with which we expect the morrow; for the health, the work, the food and the bright skies that make our lives delightful; for our friends in all parts of the earth.

Give us courage and gaiety and the quiet mind. Spare to us our friends, soften to us our enemies. Bless us, if it may be, in all our innocent endeavors. If it may not, give us the strength to endure that which is to come that we may be brave in peril, constant in tribulation, temperate in wrath and in all changes of fortune, and down to the gates of death, loyal and loving to one another. As the clay to the potter, as the windmill to the wind, as children of their parent, we beseech of you this help and mercy for Christ's sake. Amen.

Give your angels charge

Augustine's (354-430) evening prayer is an all-time favorite.

Watch, dear Lord, with those who wake or watch or weep tonight, and give your angels charge over those who sleep. Tend your sick ones, O Lord Christ. Rest your weary ones. Bless your dying ones. Soothe your suffering ones. Pity your afflicted ones. Shield your joyous ones. And all for your love's sake. Amen

Brightness be about our beds

The origin of this old family prayer is not known. It is from Mary Tileston Wilder's *Prayers Ancient and Modern* (Grosset and Dunlap, 1897 and 1928), published originally by Little, Brown and Company.

Almighty God, whose light is of eternity and knows no setting, shine forth and be our safeguard through the night; and though the earth be wrapped in darkness and the heavens be veiled from our sight, let your brightness be about our beds, and your peace within our souls, and your loving blessing upon our sleep this night. Amen.

Prayers for children

Helen Zacharias Kruger, Kitchener, Ontario, remembers praying this as a child. The *Youth Hymnary* (Faith and Life Press, 1956) identifies Luise Hensel (1798-1876) as its author and sets it to the music of a German folk tune (No. 77). The translation of the first two verses is by Marlin Jeschke (b. 1929), who grew up in Waldheim, Saskatchewan, and is now professor of philosophy and religion at Goshen College. The remaining English verses are from the *Youth Hymnary*.

Müde bin ich

Müde bin ich, geh zur Ruh,
Schliesse meine Augen zu.
Vater, lass die Augen Dein
Über meinem Bette sein!

Hab ich Unrecht heut' getan,
Sieh es, treuer Gott, nicht an!
Deine Gnad' und Jesu Blut
Machen allen Schaden gut.

Alle, die mir sind verwandt,
Gott, lass ruhn in Deiner Hand;
Allen Menschen, gross und klein,
Sollen dir befohlen sein.

Kranken Herzen sende Ruh,
Nasse Augen schliesse zu;
Lass, die noch im Finstern gehn,
Bald den Stern der Weisen sehn!

Tired, I rest at close of day,
Close my eyes, Father, and pray,
May your ever watchful eye
Guard the bed on which I lie.

Have I evil done today,
I pray, dear Lord, do not repay.
May your grace through Jesus' blood
Turn all evil into good.

All our loved ones everywhere,
Lord, we give them to thy care;
All mankind, the great and small,
Let thy love surround them all.

To the suffering ones be near;
Wipe away the mourner's tear;
Weary travelers in the night,
Lead them to eternal light.

We used the following evening prayers (from sources unknown) in our home when our children were small.

O holy Father, I thank you for all the blessings of this day. Forgive me that which I have done wrong. Bless me and keep me through the night. Amen.

Love takes care of us

Thank you, dear God, for the beautiful day,
For home and for care and for happy play.
Thank you for rest when the day is done
And love that takes care of us, every one.
Amen.

In safety sleep

May we in safety sleep tonight,
From every danger free;
Because the darkness and the light
Are both alike to Thee.

And when the rising sun displays
His cheerful beams abroad,
Then shall our grateful voice of praise
Declare thy goodness, Lord. Amen.

Beauty everywhere

The following words can be sung to the tune of "Day Is Dying in the West.")

Lord, the evening hour has come,
And we pause within our home,
Thanking you for blessings here,
And for beauties everywhere
        that bring us joy.
Holy, holy, holy, Father of all,
Happy hearts and loving ways
Help us all to tell your praise
        through every day. Amen.

Arms of love

Carolyn Harder Voth (b. 1944), Meno, Oklahoma, daughter of Waldo and Abbie Ann Harder, remembers two evening prayers from her childhood. She and John now use them with their own children—Roger, Greg, Philip, Matthew, and Rachel. Source of the first prayer is unknown.

Watch o'er your little child tonight,
Blest Savior from above,
And keep me till the morning light
Within your arms of love.

Tender shepherd

Mary Lundie Duncan (1814-1840) wrote this evening prayer for a child.

Jesus, tender shepherd, hear me;
    Bless your little lamb tonight.
Through the darkness please be near me.
    Keep me safe till morning light.

All this day your hand has led me,
    And I thank you for your care.
You have clothed and warmed and fed me.
    Listen to my evening prayer.

Let my sins be all forgiven!
    Bless the friends I love so well!
Take me, when I die, to heaven;
    Happy, there with you to dwell.

While my heart is tender

Carolyn Harder Voth says that in her family they used this prayer, part of the nineteenth century heritage of gospel songs, at bedtime in her early teen years. John Burton (1803–1877), a Congregationalist deacon and Sunday school teacher in England, published *One Hundred Original Hymns for the Young* in 1850, of which this prayer is one.

Savior, while my heart is tender,
    I would yield my heart to thee;
All my powers to thee surrender,
    Thine and only thine to be.
Take me now, Lord Jesus, take me;
    Let my youthful heart be thine;
Thy devoted servant make me;
    Fill my soul with love divine.
Send me, Lord, where thou wilt send me,
    Only do thou guide my way;
May thy grace through life attend me,
    Gladly then shall I obey.
Thine I am, O Lord, forever,
    To thy service set apart;
Suffer me to leave thee never;
    Seal thine image on my heart.

Table graces

"Then he took a loaf of bread, and when he had given thanks, he broke it. . . ." Luke 22:19

Fruits of the earth

Cara Ulrich, Archbold, Ohio, wrote down the favorite table prayer of her father, Phil Frey (1896-1984), a minister in the Mennonite churches of Fulton County, Ohio, for over forty years. The pronouns have been made contemporary.

For the fruits of the earth, our Father, as a token of your love and care for us, we pause to give you thanks. We pray you, grant that as we eat of this food, our bodies may be strengthened; and that as we fellowship together, we might be mutually benefited and your name honored and glorified. To this end, bless us and make us a blessing. For Jesus' sake, in whose name we pray. Amen.

Table spread

This was the standard table prayer of my father, Monroe Sommers (1896-1978), Plevna, Indiana. Toward the end of his life he added, "Bless our children and grandchildren."

Our Father, we thank you that you have watched over and cared for us throughout this day [night]. We thank you for the privilege of surrounding this table spread with the comforts of life. Bless it to the use of our bodies, both spiritual and temporal. Watch over us, guide and care for us, and when done with us here on this earth and the cares of earth, receive us unto yourself. In Jesus' name, we ask it. Amen.

Sustain us

James H. Everson of Bradenton, Florida, remembers that his grandmother, Marian Andrews, Syracuse, New York, taught him this prayer as a boy. He and his wife have continued to use it over the years.

Our Father in heaven,
Sustain our bodies with this food,
Our hearts with true friendship,
And our souls with your truth.
For Jesus' sake. Amen.

Bless this meal

Henry Poettcker (b. 1925), president of Mennonite Biblical Seminary, Elkhart, Indiana, remembers this simple traditional prayer from his childhood home.

Vater, segne diese Speise.
Uns zur Kraft und dir zum Preise.

Father, bless this meal,
To our strength and your praise.
Amen.

Be our guest

Helen Zacharias Kruger, Kitchener, Ontario, says that her father-in-law, Isaac Kruger (1895-1984), Dalmeny, Saskatchewan, used the following grace every morning.

Komm, Herr Jesus, Sei Du unser Gast
Und segne was Du uns bescheret hast.

Come, Lord Jesus, be our guest,
And bless what you have provided for us.
Amen.

All eyes look to you

People who grew up in the Goessel, Kansas, community remember grandparents who used a table grace from Psalm 145:15,16.

Aller Augen warten auf dich; und du gibst ihnen ihre Speise zu seiner Zeit.

Du tust deine Hand auf, und erfüllest alles, was lebet, mit Wohlgefallen. Amen.

The eyes of all look to you,
     and you give them their food in due season.
You open your hand,
     satisfying the desire of every living thing. Amen.

To work and serve

In the library of P. J. Wedel, an early professor at Bethel College, North Newton, Kansas, was a book, *Grace Before Meals*, compiled by A. William Nyce and Hubert Bunyea and published by the John Winston Company in 1911. The following three graces are from their collection. The language has been updated.

We thank you, Father, for the measure of health and strength we have, wherewith to do our daily work and to serve you. Keep us healthful, useful, and faithful. For the Christ's sake. Amen.

Fresh tokens of love

Lord, another day has brought forth fresh tokens of your great love for us. Bless the opportunities of this day, and the food wherewith we are made strong to serve you. These and all favors, we ask in Jesus' name. Amen.

Receive true bread

Grant, O Lord, as we take this food with thankfulness, we may also receive the true bread of life, your son Jesus Christ our Lord. Amen.

Black mother's prayer

Esther Mae Eby Long, Goshen, Indiana, says, " 'A Black Mother's Prayer' meant so much to our Illinois women and was often prayed at Women's Missionary and Service Commission. Essie Hawkins, the author of this prayer, is from Rehobeth, Illinois."

As we bow our heads with one accord,
We thank you for our blessing, Lord.
For change of season, sun, and rain,
That makes the growth of golden grain.
Bless this food to make our bodies strong.
Bless our minds to know the right from wrong.
Help us to be friends indeed
To all, no matter what their creed.
Teach us to live unselfishly,
Thankfully and courageously.
Praise God.
Praise God.
Praise God.
Amen.

Being loved and wanted

Thomas G. Simons is director of worship for the Catholic Diocese of Grand Rapids, Michigan. His table blessing is from *Blessings for God's People* (Ave Maria Press, 1983).

O God, bless this morning [noon, evening] meal and give to us the grace of your presence, that we may help those with whom we eat to experience the uniqueness of being loved and wanted by you, O Christ, and by those who express your love. Amen.

Table prayers for children

John and Carolyn Harder Voth's children, Inola, Oklahoma, use the following prayer.

We thank you, Lord, for your great love.
We thank you for this food.
We pray that it will make us strong
To do what's right and good. Amen.

Our children used the following three prayers at table when they were young. The second prayer is adapted from John Wesley (1703-1791).

Love be with us at our table.
May the food upon our board
Strengthen us and make us able
To do work for you, O Lord. Amen.

Be present at our table, Lord.
Be here and everywhere adored.
Bless this our food and grant that we
May feast forevermore with thee. Amen.

Thank you for the world so sweet.
Thank you for the food we eat.
Thank you for the birds that sing.
Thank you, God, for everything.

Here are three more table prayers for children. The first was found in the papers of Pauline Krehbiel Raid (1907-1984), Bluffton, Ohio. Sources for all three are unknown.

We thank you, Lord, for happy hearts,
    For rain and sunny weather.
We thank you, Lord, for this our food,
    And that we are together. Amen.

For health and food,
For love and friends,
For everything
Your goodness sends,
Father in heaven,
We thank you. Amen.

Dear God, we thank you for this food
And other blessings too,
And as you give, so may we share
The good things sent by you. Amen.

All good gifts

Muriel Thiessen Stackley, Newton, Kansas, and Mary Pankratz Rempel, Hesston, Kansas, recall this German grace from their childhood.

Alle gute Gaben,
Alles was wir haben,
Kommt, O Herr, von dir.
Dank sei dir dafür. Amen.

All good gifts,
Everything that we have,
Come, O Lord, from you.
Thank you. Amen.

Bread on every table

Miriam Housman, Lancaster, Pennsylvania, found this prayer in a Mennonite children's paper in the early 1960s. She has used it with kindergarten children for many years, and when doing a special service project for a particular country adds the name of the country at the end, as "especially in [name of country]."

Dear God,
I gratefully bow my head
To thank you for my daily bread,
And may there be a goodly share
On every table everywhere. Amen.

Special occasions

Do not worry about anything, but in everything
by prayer and supplication with thanksgiving
let your requests be made known to God.
Philippians 4:6

Sunday morning

The following prayer is taken from Walter Rauschenbush's book *For God and the People, Prayers of the Social Awakening* **(1909). See note on page 8.**

O God, we rejoice that today no burden of work will be upon us and that our body and soul are free to rest. We thank you that of old, this day was hallowed by you for all who toil, and that from generation to generation the weary sons and daughters of humankind have found it a shelter and a breathing space. We pray for your peace on all our brothers and sisters who are glad to cease from labor and to enjoy the comfort of their homes and the companionship of those whom they love. Forbid that the pressure of covetousness or thoughtless love of pleasure rob any who are worn of their divine right of rest.

Grant us wisdom and self-control that our pleasures may not be follies, lest our leisure drain us more than our work. Teach us that in the mystic unity of our nature our body cannot rest unless our soul has repose, so that we may walk this day in your presence in tranquility of spirit, taking each joy as your gift, and on the morrow return to our labor refreshed and content. Amen.

Another Sunday prayer

For Christmas in 1937, Emanuel Bontrager (b. 1921), now a grandfather himself, received from his Amish grandparents, Emanuel and Barbara Hochstedler of rural Kokomo, Indiana, a small red prayer book. *Book of Prayers for Everybody and All Occasions* **was published by Geo. W. Noble in Chicago in 1907. This prayer is taken from that book.**

We thank you for this day of rest. The week has gone quickly on its round, making our hearts once more glad in its light. Help us to improve its hours wisely.

Grant us some share in the chorus of praise that ascends this day to your throne, following the sun in its round of the earth; some part in the labor and service of your people; some portion of the inheritance of those who call the Sabbath a delight. May we keep this day holy to the end thereof, that the remembrance of it may cause us joy and not pain or misgivings. May the day help onward our pilgrimage toward the Sabbath of rest which remains for the people of God. In the name of our Lord Jesus, we pray. Amen.

Sunday evening

See note about Walter Rauschenbusch, author of this prayer, on page 8.

O Lord, we lift our souls to you in the awe of the eventide. We rejoice that in the quiet of your day of rest our spirits have been attuned to the melodies of your beauty. We bless you for every word of solemn truth which has entered our hearts, for every touch of loving hand that has comforted us, for every opportunity we have had to speak some message from our heart to the heart of our brothers and sisters.

Forgive us if any hours have been wasted on profitless things that have brought us no satisfaction, or if we have dragged our dusty cares into your sacred day and made the holy common. We pray for your blessing on all who have come near to us this day, on all who have brought us strength, on all who are sad and hungry for you, on all your great humanity in its sin and beauty. May our last waking thought be a benediction for our fellows and in our sleep may we still be with you. Amen.

Advancing years

Ruth Kortemeier, Goshen, Indiana, says the following prayer is one of her favorites. "I am a senior citizen and have it pasted in the front of my Bible." Sources disagree concerning the dates of Alathea Grenfell, whether 1829-1923 or 1846-1932, but agree that she wrote the prayer when she was in her 90s.

O Father of mercies and God of all comfort, our only help in time of need, I come to you for help to meet the trials of advancing years. Give me courage, and patience to bear the infirmities, privations, and loneliness of old age. Help me to fight successfully its temptations to be exacting, selfish, unreasonable, irritable, and complaining. Preserve my mental faculties unimpaired to the end, keep my heart and affections warm so that I may never fail to sympathize with the joys, sorrows, and interests of others, and to be deeply grateful for the love and forbearance of those about me.

And so fit and prepare me against the hour of death that I may be able to face it fearlessly, trusting in your promise to be with me as I pass through the dark valley so that, departing in peace, my soul may be received into your everlasting kingdom, through Jesus Christ, my Lord and Savior. Amen.

Family reunion

See the note about Walter Rauschenbusch, the author of this prayer, on page 8.

O Lord, our hearts are full of gratitude and praise, for after the long days of separation you have brought us together again to look into the dear faces and read their love as of old. As the happy memories of the years when we were young together rise up to cheer us, may we feel anew how closely our lives were wrought into one another in their early making, and what a treasure we have had in our home. Whatever new friendships we may form, grant that the old loves may abide to the end and grow ever sweeter with the ripening years. Amen.

Family finances

When in her late 80s Lillian Lantz Rich Sprunger of Washington, Illinois, and Bluffton, Ohio, called together her three children and their spouses to discuss family finances, she first led them in this prayer which she had written.

Dear Father of us all, we come to you today in praise and gratitude for all your great and beautiful creation, for all blessings you have bestowed on each of us here. For each of our children, their spouses, our grandchildren, and great-grandchildren, we thank you.

Now as our small family group assembles today to discuss family economic problems that may arise in the future, we ask your ever-present guidance today and always as decisions need to be made. Keep us ever mindful that you are the source of all wisdom, and that we need only to listen quietly at times until your plan is our plan, your love for us becomes our love for each other.

We thank you for all guidance you have given us in the past and for all we will receive today and in the future. Amen.

Outlook the mark of time

Rufus Ellis (1819-1885) recognizes that both the living and the dead are one family in Christ.

We thank you for the dear and faithful dead, for those who have made the distant heavens a home for us and whose truth and beauty are even now in our hearts. One by one you gather the scattered families out of the earth light into the heavenly glory, from the distractions and strife and weariness of time to the peace of eternity.

We thank you for the labors and the joys of these mortal years. We thank you for our deep sense of the mysteries that lie beyond our dust, and for the eye of faith which you have opened for all who believe in your son to outlook that mark. May we live altogether in your faith and love, and in that hope which is full of immortality. Amen.

Childbirth

I wrote this prayer before the birth of one of our children.

How I praise you for the life within me, the fruit of our love, for the mysterious way in which you have used my body during the past nine months. I have not created with my mind or will, saying, "Today I shall make the legs, tomorrow the eyes." I have but committed my body to you, the great Creator.

I offer to you this tiredness of limb.

As the day of birth approaches, I ask that I may labor well. Praise, honor, glory to you forever. Amen.

Parents for their children

This is another prayer from the Amish *Ernsthafte Christenpflicht*. See note on page 4.

Dear God and Father, Creator and Guardian of all living beings, give us the grace to bring up our children in the nurture and admonition of the Lord. Help us to be an example of all virtue. Give our children grace and the gifts of the Spirit so they will profit from the admonitions we give them. Kindle in them the true fear of God, which is the beginning of all wisdom. Fill them with the desire to do your will and to claim your promises.

Favor them with true knowledge and keep them from all idolatry and false teachings. May they learn to know the true faith and to practice all godly virtues, remaining steadfast unto the end. Give them a faithful and obedient mind, with true wisdom and understanding. Let them increase in wisdom and stature, and in favor with God and other people.

Implant in their hearts a fervent love for your Holy Word. May they be attentive to prayer and devotions, respectful toward the ministers and toward everyone, honest and upright in all their doings. Help them to show love and forbearance to all. Protect them from the evil influence of this world, so they will not be led astray by evil companions.

May they never indulge in evil, nor give offense to others. Be a shield unto them in all kinds of danger lest they be overtaken by a violent or untimely death. Let your church here on earth be preserved and enlarged by us, our children and descendants. Finally, may we all meet in the celestial heavens, with the innumerable multitudes, with palm leaves in our hands, to sing the new song with joy and praise to you forever. This we pray in Jesus' name. Amen.

Mother for her daughter

For information about Pauline Raid, the writer of this prayer, see page 11.

Lord Jesus, we pray for Elizabeth Ann. Help her to find that discipline by which alone life can be successfully lived and character achieved. May she learn that just as steam is effective when contained in the walls of a cylinder, so will youthful energies be effective when controlled. We ask you to protect her physically. Throw around her the golden aura of your protecting presence. Be her teacher and her guide. Send into her life the especially chosen companions and friends you want her to have. Save her from any costly blunders that would haunt her down the years. Give to her that joy and happiness that will enable her to go out to meet life, bearing with her those lasting satisfactions which only you can bestow. We thank you, Lord. Amen.

After a quarrel

For information about Lillian Lantz Rich Sprunger, from whom this prayer comes, see page 45.

O Prince of Peace, bring quietness to our spirits that we may consider the cause of our disagreement in the clear light of reason.

Forgive our hastiness, our impatience, and our desire to hurt each other in the heat of argument.

Help us not to harbor bitterness nor resentment, nor to remember carefully every harsh word which has been spoken.

Grant us the spirit of compassionate understanding, and help us realize that our discipleship demands forgiveness until "seventy times seven."

In turning to you in prayer, may we find our petty strife rebuked by the thought of your redeeming love. Amen.

Understanding another

Josephine Moffett Benton (b. 1905) is a Quaker writer long associated with Pendle Hill, a Quaker education center in Wallingford, Pennsylvania. This is from *Gift of a Golden String* published by the United Church Press in 1963.

Lord, I thank you for the miracle of personality, and I pray that when I do not comprehend a loved one, you, Lord, will tender my heart, quiet my tongue, inform my mind, give me courtesy and sensitivity of spirit. Amen.

For missionaries

The Third Presbyterian Church of Rochester, New York, published *A Sheaf of Prayers* by Paul Moore Strayer in 1926.

Dear Father, we thank you for home-staying loves, loves that find the objects in the home, the church, the community. We thank you too for far-traveling loves, loves that find their objects in the big world, loves to which the world is a neighborhood and humankind a family. We pray for those who, driven by far-traveling loves, go even to the uttermost parts of the earth to tell the story of God's love as it is in Christ Jesus. We pray that they may be upheld, strengthened and comforted by our prayers, our sympathies, and our hopes. We pray that they may find favor with all the people and may go in and out among them, approved of all, loved of all. May they show the love of God both by their lives and by their teachings. May those among whom they work find in our religion not the destruction but the fulfillment of their own, as the sun fulfills the morning star. May your kingdom come and your will be done on earth as it is in heaven. We ask it in Christ's name. Amen.

Thanksgiving for trees

Marguerite Harmon Bro was an educational missionary in China from 1919 to 1925. This prayer appeared in *Prayers of Women* by Lisa Sergio (Harper and Row, 1965) and in *Everyday a Prayer* (Harper, 1943)

Our Father, we thank you for trees! We thank you for the trees of our childhood in whose shade we played and read and dreamed; for the trees of our school days, the trees along the paths where friendship walked. We thank you for special trees which will always stand large in our memory because for some reason of our own they became our trees. We thank you for the great stretches of trees which make the forests. May we always stand humbly before your trees and draw strength from them as they, in their turn, draw sustenance from your bounties of earth and sun and air. Amen.

Christmas kin

The following prayer, from an unknown writer, is from the Noble book. See note on page 42.

Blessed Jesus, Savior of humankind, may we continually honor you and graciously serve you,
By remembering our kinship with everyone,
By well wishing, friendly speaking and kindly doing,
By cheering the downcast and adding sunshine to daylight,
By welcoming strangers (poor shepherds or wise men),
By keeping the music of the angels' song in this home.
God help us every one to spread abroad the blessings of Jesus,
In whose name we keep Christmas. Amen.

Work for the new year

Grant Stoltzfus (1916-1974), beloved teacher-writer-historian-churchman, wrote this prayer for the year 1951.

O God, we thank you as another year comes on. Teach us to number our days during this year so that we may apply ourselves unto good works and wisdom. There will be much to do this year: children we should teach, homes we should enter, schools we should visit and houses of worship that call us to enter, pray, and serve. There will be much for us to do in the busy home, on the farm, and at the desk.

May we do all in the name of Jesus. May we be willing to work long and hard and to leave the results to you. May we do all things decently and in order and with good will in our hearts—even the love of Christ—so that we will forgive when necessary. Save us from sin—the sin of self-seeking—as we go about our work. Make us always mindful that it is your work and not ours that we would do. In the name of Christ. Amen.

Special times for children

New year

This prayer came from a thirteen-year-old boy.

We thank you, God, for the new year. We thank you for keeping us last year. Forgive us our sins. Help there to be peace on earth. Amen.

New baby

This prayer and the next were prayed by our children when they were small.

Thank you for our new baby brother [sister]. Help us to take good care of him [her]. Amen.

First day at school

Dear God,
Thank you that I can go to school.
Help me to learn things and to have friends. Amen.

Birthday

This prayer was written by an Indian boy.

Dear Jesus,
Help me to be just like you were,
When you were as old as I am now.

In the congregation

Praise the Lord.
I will give thanks to the Lord with my whole heart,
in the company of the upright, in the congregation.

Psalm 111:1 (Revised Standard Version)

Open our eyes of faith

Harry Yoder (b. 1904) has held pastorates in Goshen, Indiana, and Carlock and Washington, Illinois.

O God, our eternal heavenly Father, we joyously come together at this time of worship, realizing that we need not summon you to be in our midst, for you are here. We need not call you to be in the secret places of our hearts, for you are there.

We need rather that our eyes of faith be opened, that we may see you; that our ears be unstopped, that we may hear you; and that our minds be made sensitive, our hearts tender, and our wills submissive, so that we may receive your ministry to us.

Grant each one present a blessing, O Lord, as each has need. We pray in the name of Jesus Christ, our Lord. Amen.

Grow from glory to glory

Arlene M. Mark, Elkhart, Indiana, is the author of *Worship Resources* (Faith and Life Press, Newton, Kansas, and Mennonite Publishing House, Scottdale, Pennsylvania, 1982).

Great God,
We adore your majesty and might
and marvel in the mercy of salvation.

We thank you that Jesus brightens our darkness
and shows us the way to righteousness.

Today, give us wisdom to grow from glory to glory
and empower us to proclaim the news of salvation
through Christ Jesus, our Lord.
Amen.

Find the center of our lives

Russell Mast (b. 1915), a graduate of Bluffton College and Hartford Theological Seminary, has held pastorates in Kansas, Ohio, Pennsylvania, and South Dakota. Although the pronouns have been changed in this prayer, Russell Mast prefers the older language for public prayer.

O God our Father, your greatness stands over all our littleness, your wisdom over our ignorance, your power over our weakness. We gather in our prayer before the brightness of your being to come under the authority of your word, that we may make all our decisions in the light of your purpose and engage ourselves in all that we do in answer to your call. We seek your presence now, that we may serve you where "sound the cries of race and clan." With you in our worship, prepare us for the days with others in work.

Deliver us, we beseech you, from lives that are self-contained, that cannot look beyond the narrow limits of self, that seek always to be served rather than to serve, to receive rather than to give. Help us to understand that only as we lose ourselves do we really find ourselves. Put windows into our souls that we may look out instead of in, that we may find the center of our lives in you, and the object of our service in others. So grant that in the living of our lives and in all that we seek to do, we may bring healing to a sick world; and that to all of our feeble efforts and broken attempts, you will add the perfection of your own hand and the fulfillment which only you can give.

O merciful Father, we pray for the peace of the world, for those whose lives are taken from them on the battlefield, on the streets, and in their homes. We pray for those who take the lives of others and for those who make decisions that others shall take the lives of others. Grant that we may see anew and dedicate ourselves anew to him who is the Prince of Peace, who preached peace, who made peace, who is our peace, and who calls us to be instruments of his peace. Help us to see the way in which the issues of peace in our world are reflected in our own souls, and grant that by the way we live, the manner in which we order our lives, and in all that we do, we may bring to life some measure of the peace which the world is seeking.

And now we wait further upon you as we continue our worship. Speak that word which is your own to the heart of each worshiper that is his or her own, and may there be patient hearing and an obedient response. Amen.

When not in joy or stress

Beulah Marner Cobb (b. 1925) gardens, loves her family, and is a longtime member of First Mennonite Church, Indianapolis, Indiana, where she used this prayer in 1974.

God,
We are gathered here to worship you,
to sing praises to you,
to hear the reading of your Word,
to listen as others tell of their lives as they
endeavor to follow you.

We all have difficulties from time to time.
These are unique opportunities to grow.
We thank you for them.
At these times we
often seek comfort and support from each other
and from you.

We also experience occasions of great joy and happiness.
We delight in sharing these events and happenings.

But often, God, we find ourselves neither in a state of joy
nor stress. We are bored or hot or irritable or in a state of
confusion or tired from long hours of work. At such times
we may not be aware of you or of our surroundings. We
confess this state of mind to you and ask for an awareness of
your constant presence.

We thank you for each person present here today.
We praise you for your great promise to supply all
of our needs. Amen.

In the dryness of August

Maynard Shelly (b. 1925), Newton, Kansas, an editor and writer, used this prayer one hot August morning in 1978 with the Bethel College congregation, North Newton, Kansas.

Dear God, we're here. We know the world is filled with many who are needy, and we would pray for them. But we know that we too are needy. We are empty, needing filling; we are dirty, needing washing; we are unruly, needing forgiving.

So we gather our thoughts and feelings; gathering ourselves to say a word of thanks, to express the gratitude that will lift us out of ourselves, to see what is outside and all around. And so we say, thank you, God.

Yes, thank you, God—but for what? In the dryness, in the heat, in the aridness of August—in this brittleness, the tension, the pressure, the dying of these days, amidst the getting nowhere-ness: yes, thank you, God—but for what?

To begin with and to make it a summing up of all: We thank you, God, for seven days in August, the seven that have passed and the seven, if it be your will, that will come. For here is the measure of what you have given us—you have given us in each day the life that cannot be taken lightly, a gift from you.

Each day is an eternity, inelastic time that goes slowly for children waiting for school to be over or a church service to end; so slowly for those waiting to be married, for those wanting reward and recognition; so slowly for those recovering from a stubborn illness or a persistent weakness of body and/or soul.

Yet each day is an eternity moving so swiftly for those who have work to do—books to write, socks to mend, pictures to paint, children to teach, bills to pay, houses to build, proposals to submit, gardens to plant.

But slow or fast, we've come to pray: dear God, we're here. Thank you, God. We come to prayer to wrestle with you, God, seeking as did Jacob, our identity and our name. We learn our name in our giving—for you, O God, are a giving God. We would be like you and learn how hard and how necessary it is to give—to give ourselves in selfless service: how really tough!

So we pray: Good God, accept our gifts. Thank you, God. Dear God, we're here. Amen.

Transformed for witness

For information about Harry Yoder, who offered this prayer, see note on page 56.

Eternal God, our heavenly Father, out of a heart and mind of love and loyalty we gather here to worship you in spirit and in truth. We know that the experience of worship draws us together in the power of your Holy Spirit. When we worship in spirit and in truth we believe that the Spirit is present to judge us, to cleanse us, to forgive us, and to unite us. We pray, O Lord, that through prayer and worship we may increase the effectiveness of our faith. May our lives be transformed into a powerful witness for you.

Now, O Lord, realizing that you know us better than we know ourselves or each other, we commit ourselves into your care and keeping. If there be those among us who are caught up in serious decision making, grant spiritual guidance and satisfaction. If there be sadness or depression, give a surge of faith and exuberance. If there be physical illness and suffering, we pray for comfort and healing, according to need and according to your will. We pray for those who are making social and cultural adjustments to new ways of life. Grant a special portion of wisdom and strength to those who are in places of authority and responsibility. Our prayer is that the light of your truth may prevail in all walks of life and that the fellowship of our worship may become the spiritual light of our community and of the world.

We pray for alertness and sensitivity among us that we might serve as your faithful ambassadors in our time and in our fellowship. We love your church and desire to make it flourish. We pray in the name of Christ. Amen.

Lay our burdens in God's hands

The author of this prayer prefers to remain anonymous.

Dear Lord, we come to you this morning, not because we are good people, but because we are sinners much in need of your forgiveness; not because we are strong, but because we are weak and much in need of your grace.

We confess our sins to you—sins of anger, hatred, envy, covetousness, self-righteousness. We confess that during the past week we failed to do what we should have done. Cleanse us from our sins, that in you we may be healed and whole. We praise you for your forgiveness which makes us indeed your children and part of your spotless church.

We bring to you also our anxieties and worries. Some of us are anxious about our health or about family members who are ill. But in you is healing and health. Some of us are anxious about members of our families who seem far from you. But you are not far from them. Some of us are anxious about financial matters or crops. Some of us are discouraged. We lay these burdens in your capable hands. Grant us the faith to believe that all will be well, that all manner of things will be well, for you have gone into the future ahead of us, ordering a pathway for each of us. As you have sustained us in the past, so you will sustain us in the future. For this we thank you.

Our hearts are sorely troubled by the evil in the world. We pray that peace may come at last in every nation everywhere. We pray for innocent people bereaved and suffering because of war. Let a new time come through your spirit, a time of truth, of justice, and of peace. Your kingdom come. Your will be done on earth as it is in heaven. Amen.

Students in Botswana

Three of Christine Habegger Purves's ninth-graders at Maun Secondary School in Gabarone, Botswana, composed the following.

You, O Lord, are the God who sees on the outside and the inside. Thank you for the true fellowship in your church. In church, there is a place for everyone. It doesn't matter how dirty or poor you are. In church, there is no difference between even our president or our headmaster and me. We can sit on the same bench, for we are praying together.

The church people love me even when I am far away. They say when I am gone I must continue to share in the services of any church I like, because people are all worshiping God. They help me know your teaching: the more you give, the more you receive. We worship you, Lord, our Great Herdsman, the only one who can keep us all together. Amen.

New year mercies

The prayers of Larry Kehler (b. 1933) were collected and placed into a book when he served as pastor of the Charleswood Mennonite Church, Winnipeg, Manitoba, from 1976 to 1980. The following two prayers are from that book. He is now executive secretary of the Conference of Mennonites in Canada.

Thank you, Lord, for the mercy of new beginnings, for opportunities to start over.

Help us to forgive ourselves and each other for our past mistakes so that we will not clutter our new starts with the effects of destructive thoughts and actions which lie behind us.

Give us a willingness to receive forgiveness.

In our minds we know that you are always quickly ready to forgive us our misdeeds and our steps in the wrong direction, but help us to accept your gracious forgiveness in our hearts so that we might experience the purifying and liberating relief of being pardoned.

We often feel guilty and useless even though we have embarked on a new path with your help.

Thank you for your continuous assurances that we do not need to remain permanently guilt-ridden and anxious.

We want to make good use of the coming year and the new decade.

Help us to be responsible stewards of whatever time is available to us.

Give us a desire to spread joy and goodness around us, to be makers of peace, to show love, and to be sources of hope in our families and neighborhoods.

Grant vitality to our congregation. We want to be spiritually alive and aware. We want to attract and welcome people who are searching for a place to belong. We want to affirm and love each other within the congregational family.

We want to stimulate and inspire our children and young people through our teaching and example. Help us to this end.

Be with those members of our fellowship who are scattered around the world. Strengthen their Christian witness in whatever they are doing.

Be present with those who are journeying back to their homes after having spent the holidays with friends and relatives. May they travel carefully and wisely.

Be with all of us as we return to our weekly routines, our studies, and our various vocations. Help us to do whatever we do with diligence and pride. Amen.

True hosannas

We whisper
    and sing
    and shout
    your praise, Lord.
Do our hosannas ring true?
We welcome you as King of kings.
Do our works and words of faith point toward
    your kingdom?
We remember how you wept over Jerusalem.
Do you now also weep for Winnipeg and Ottawa?
    for Toronto and Vancouver, for Edmonton and
    Montreal?
We praise you on this Sunday of Palms.
Will we have forgotten you by Friday—
    the Friday of your execution?
We have no palm branches to wave;
    we do not have the freedom
    or the courage to shout hosanna.
Help us nevertheless to take what we have
    to lay before you as you enter our lives
    anew with news so good and so different we hardly
    know what to make of it.
Help us to take all that we have, of time, talent,
    possessions or energy to glorify you today and
    every day. Amen.

Easter overcomes

Paul Moore Strayer composed this prayer. See note on page 50.

We thank you, Lord, for the faith which overcomes the world. We thank you for victory over life with its disappointments, its failures, and its separations; that the dominant note of life is joy and its mightiest force is love and its last word is hope. We thank you that in many a gray morning we have seen the stone rolled away from the heart sepulchers and an angel sitting on it; so that the sorrow and loss which seemed to have closed down upon us was not only rolled back but glorified, and what seemed an irreparable loss has become a guide. We thank you for the victory over life.

We thank you too for the victory over death; that the tomb cannot hold our dead nor the grave enclose our beloved. We do not know how you could bring them forth. We do not know how you can lead these broken lives and severed loves of ours to the fulfillment they demand, but all we know of love in ourselves, all we see of it in other human hearts, makes us confident that you will this fulfillment make, and what you will you can do. Yours, O Lord, is the victory.

We thank you that in the light of Easter, even death, that was the king of terrors, has become a hallowed thing, the answer to our prayer for life, more life and fuller. Help us to think of death not as the end of being but as its true beginning; not as a wall against which we dash our heads but as a door opening to a larger room in the Father's house, a room prepared for us and made homelike by those who have gone before. Amen.

Going back to school

James Dunn (b. 1941) is a pastor of the First Mennonite Church, Newton, Kansas, and was formerly director of higher education for the General Conference Mennonite Church.

As our prayers surround the persons in our congregation going back to school this week and in the weeks to come, we ask, God:

that your presence might go before them to select and illumine their paths;

that your spirit might empower them to seek and know your truth;

that your peace might dwell in them, comforting and marking the way.

As they go, so do we. We commit to them our faithful prayers. We share with them our mutual counsel and admonition as we wrestle with life's difficult issues. We encourage them through financial support of our public and church schools.

Help us, we pray to make today's commitment with our students going back to school tomorrow's reality. Source of all knowledge, help us to seek you in our search for truth. May we seek not just life's facts, but your acts for us as we serve you, who are the way, the truth, and the life. In Jesus' name we pray. Amen.

College discipleship

Judy Stutzman Kanagy (b. 1959), as instructor in health, physical education, and recreation at Bluffton College, used this prayer at the annual faculty retreat in August 1984.

Lord, the beginning of a new school year brings mixed emotions. We come together again as a little child boldly approaches her father, in love and need. You are our father. We come to you confidently, worshipfully, penitently, joyfully, airing our doubts, our fears, our problems and needs, knowing that you hear us and that you rejoice in the faith of your children.

This assembly is charged with leading an important part of your church, the students. The young, impressionable, wide open minds absorb what we say and do. Help us to lead personal and professional lives which are free from hypocrisy. We need to demonstrate clearly your love in our own lives so that we do not introduce a pathetic mishmash that becomes a stumbling block to those who are seeking you. Help us to be leaders who show that discipleship, servanthood, idealism, hope, and faith are exemplified by Christ. Help us to show that the gospel is possible in this day and age.

In our rush to make a point, convince, prove, we talk and brandish arguments, strike hard to reach the imagination or the emotions. But like a child who angrily pounds and kicks a locked door, trying desperately to move it, to open it, and then peers into the keyhole only to find it blocked, we sometimes despair.

Grant, Lord, that we may learn to wait reverently, loving and praying in silence, standing in hope until the door to the humanly impossible is opened. In Christ's name we pray. Amen.

Thanksgiving

John Rempel (b. 1944) was chaplain at Conrad Grebel College, Waterloo, Ontario. He is now a pastor in New York.

Lord God, you are the king of the universe.
We see no change in your goodness from one generation to the next.
You let rain fall on the just and the unjust.
We praise you that you never give up loving us and our world.

Today we thank you:
> that we may gather to worship you without fear or intimidation;

that fruit and grain have ripened to give us
> food for another year;

for people who have entered our lives and
> taught us to love, hope, and dream;

for strong minds and bodies that can make our
> world more human;

for our queen [president] and a social order
> where fairness, individuality, and dissent have a place;

for salvation now and eternal life in your presence.

We pray for those who suffer when creation breaks down;
> people without harvests, without lovers,
> with minds that despair of bringing change.

Be merciful, O God,
> to everyone everywhere for whom life has broken down.

And push us to be merciful.

Accept our thanks, we pray, for Jesus' sake. Amen.

Psa. 117

Late autumn

Chizuko Kawamoto (b. c.1948) was a student at the International Christian University, Mitaka, Tokyo, Japan. She used this prayer in a worship service in the university church on Thanksgiving Sunday, November 20, 1966.

O God, our Father in heaven,
On this clear and calm day of late autumn,
We pray you that this day
    may begin with your light,
    may be filled with your love,
    and may conclude with your blessing.

In these days of noise and confusion,
    give us peace and tolerance.
We are weak people who often take a false step.
By your mighty hand,
    lead us into the land of righteousness. Amen.

Night before Christmas

Melvin D. Schmidt (b. 1937) was born in Kansas, graduated from Bethel College and Yale Divinity School, and has had pastorates in Kansas and Ohio.

Our Father:

who has been very much with us from very
ancient times when Immanuel meant simply:
a child is born,

who has sought to enter the lives of your people
even when they turned their backs to you,
or when they told you there was no room to be born
or when you had to flee the jealous wrath of kings,

We thank you tonight

that you have brought us to this time and place
where we can share in word and deed and music
the glorious truth of your overcoming and
overpowering light,
where we can share once more
the height and depth of your great love,
where we can celebrate what it means
to be the people upon whom
you have set your irrepressible love,
where we can remind each other that
you are now
as you have always been,
that today there is nothing we can do
nor anything that can happen
to keep you from being born among us. Amen.

Born on Christmas

This prayer comes from Paul Moore Strayer. (See page 50.) It echoes the mood of the first four lines of *Cherubinischer Wandersmann* by Angelus Silesius (1624–1677), a German poet whose real name was Johannes Scheffler: "Though Christ a thousand times/ In Bethlehem be born,/ If he's not born in you,/ Your soul is still forlorn."

Our Father, we come to you at this season when heaven approached nearest to earth and ask that we may make more room in our lives for heaven. We are already embarked on the great business of heaven, doing for others in forgetfulness of self. Confirm us in that business, O Lord. May it become a habit which shall hold over into the new year. Help us in the holy conspiracy for others' happiness.

May we make a place in our hearts for the Lord Christ, there to rule and reign. May we not crowd him out as he was crowded out of the inn the night he was born. Though Christ in Bethlehem a thousand times be born, if he's not born in us, we are all forlorn.

May he be born in us, O God. Give us the spirit of a little child. Give us the wonder of a child, wonder which is nearly akin to worship. Give us the faith of a child, the simple faith of the shepherds, who heard angel voices in the Syrian sky.

Give us the trust of a child, the deep trust of the wise men, who followed the star until it stood over the place where the young child lay. May we all together worship the Babe of Bethlehem. Amen.

Baptized into a family

Clifford Lind (b. 1933), Eugene, Oregon, used this prayer at the baptism of his son Carl in 1984.

Our God, we pray that Carl will always find fulfillment, peace, and joy in his decision to accept you as Lord. We rejoice that he has chosen to make public that decision this day. We pray that he will find in the relationship with you:

strength to resist evil,

courage to follow your way,

humility to acknowledge error.

We thank you for our congregation and for the larger church which have provided nurture for him. We pray that he will experience within the church family:

support when burdens are heavy,

mutual forgiveness and reconciliation,

assistance in times of need,

nurture and worship in frequent gatherings,

mutual sharing of joys and sorrow.

We pray that Carl's participation in the church will be an expression of love, service, and joy. We pray that, in the larger society, his life will demonstrate peace, compassion, and love. Amen.

Peace and salvation

At the invitation of Pope John Paul II, Christians from thirty Christian world communions gathered in the medieval city of Assisi, Italy, on October 27, 1986, for a day of prayer for peace. On that occasion, Paul Kraybill (b. 1925), executive secretary, Mennonite World Conference, used the following prayer. Source of the prayer is not known.

Lord Jesus Christ, you stretched out your arms of love on the hard wood of the cross that everyone might come within the reach of your saving embrace; so clothe us in your Spirit, that we, reaching forth our hands in love, may bring those who do not know you to the knowledge and love of you, for the honor of your holy name. Amen.

Make wars cease

Jim Stutzman Amstutz (b. 1954), campus pastor at Bluffton College, Bluffton, Ohio, offered this prayer based on Psalm 46 on April 30, 1987, on the occasion of a lecture on peace.

God, you are our refuge and strength,
our ever present help in trouble.
Therefore, we have no cause to fear,
  though the earth be obsessed with war,
  though the waters of hopelessness roar and foam,
  and the foundations of shalom be shaken.
There is a river of righteousness and justice,
  whose streams make glad the place where you dwell.
Because you have covenanted with us,
  we know that you will not fail us.

Nations rise up against nations, claiming ultimate power.
Governments fall at the hands and arms of others.
Yet your Word lives and is not overcome.
One day
    you shall make wars cease to the ends of the earth.
One day
    you shall break the rifle and shatter the handgun.
One day
    you shall recycle the tank,
    the submarine,
    the missile,
    and the bomb.
May we now
    Be still and know that you are God.
You will be exalted among the nations.
You will be exalted in the earth.
Only you,
    Lord Almighty, are worthy of our allegiance.
Only you,
    can be our fortress.
Though they kill the body,
they cannot kill the soul.
We pray this in the name of the one you sent into the world
as the Prince of Peace.
    But the world knew him not.
The one who overcame evil with good,
    who died so that we might live—
    even Jesus Christ, our Lord. Amen.

At close of worship

For information about Harry Yoder, who wrote this prayer, see note on page 56.

Eternal God, our father, by whose power we are created and by whose love we are redeemed, as we go from this hour of worship, guide and strengthen us by your Spirit, that we may give ourselves to your service and live all our days in love to one another and to you, through Jesus Christ our Lord. Amen.

Hide your word

Lloyd Neve went to Japan in 1948 as a missionary with the American Lutheran Church. He taught Old Testament for many years at the Japan Lutheran Theological College, Tokyo.

Help us to hide your word in our hearts.
May it be a fire in us leading to action. Amen.

Invocation for a wedding

Esko Loewen (1917-1981), held pastorates in Indiana, Pennsylvania, and Kansas.

O God, our Father, source of infinite love, bless us with a sense of your indwelling presence as we worship here. Keep us sensitive to the wonder of things which fill our days and give meaning to life. Deepen in us the level of our loving.

Especially do we pray your divine blessing on these two who come here in this high moment of their lives. Be near them as they make their promises to each other, that they shall pledge their vows with deepest sincerity.

And grant to us all, we pray, a heightened sense of the joy of life because we share this moment with them, in your loving spirit. Amen.

Wedding anniversary

Burton G. Yost (b. 1928), professor of religion at Bluffton College, used this prayer at the fiftieth anniversary of Warren and Helen Rosenberger, Toledo, Ohio, on August 12, 1978.

O God, our heavenly Father,
>we thank you that in your wisdom and providence
>you have set us in families,

so that we find our completion in another person,
when a man and a woman hold to each other in love
>and faithfulness and thus become one—
>a union to be dissolved only by another part
>of your wisdom and providence.

We thank you that in that union men and women find
>so many of your blessings,
>that the struggles and difficulties
>of life together
>produce so many good fruits.

We thank you, heavenly Father, that these things
>have been true for Warren and Helen.

By your providence they were brought together,
>and by your providence,
>they have been sustained and nourished.

Your grace has granted them many good things—
>a child to love and care for;
>and now grandchildren for whom to do the same;
>good families and friends with whom to share
>and from whom to receive;
>worthy occupations by which to serve others;
>good health and recovery from sickness;
>and a continuous love and respect for each other.

We thank you for all the goodness of these fifty years
>and ask that your blessings continue
>with them in the years ahead.

As your love is steadfast and unfailing, O Lord,
   grant that their love to you and to each other
   may abide and that in that faithfulness the
   years ahead may be even more blessed.
May your blessing also rest upon all
   who love Warren and Helen.
We pray this in the name of Jesus Christ our Lord.
Amen.

Church council meeting

Elnore Rosenberger Yost (b, 1927), Bluffton, Ohio, used this prayer at the beginning of a church council meeting in 1982.

Our heavenly Father,
we come before you this evening as your people.
Help us to put on those things that the Scripture tells us to put on—compassion, kindness, humility, gentleness, patience—and above all, to put on love, which binds us together in harmony.

As we report, talk, and discuss, may we feel your Spirit, so that what we do may be done in the name of the Lord Jesus.

We are here this evening to plan and work so that our church may draw people to you and to your mission. Help us to think how we really can do this. Help us to use our financial resources, our time, energy, and abilities to that end. We pray that we may work together in a way that will uplift and encourage one another.

We thank you for our church and for the faith and service of our people. May the word of Christ dwell richly in us all.

We give thanks to you, O God, for your salvation, for your forgiveness, for your Word, and for your guidance. In Jesus' name. Amen.

Workday at church

All day the church women had rolled bandages, run sewing machines, quilted, and knotted comforters. At the end of their workday they were led in this prayer by Lillian Lantz Rich Sprunger.

Dear Father of us all, we come to you at the close of this afternoon session in deep gratitude for your guiding hand, for a unified spirit in the work done, but most of all for the challenges brought to us today. May we accept them joyously and humbly, conscientiously and faithfully.

Keep us ever conscious that our calling is a high calling, not only here and in our homes and communities, but even unto the uttermost parts of the earth.

Teach us to use wisely and unselfishly the power you have given us, the wisdom to plan our homework so that we do not become slaves to it. But on the other hand, teach us to so lose ourselves in the tasks of each day that we never give in to self-pity or boredom.

May we strive always to see the good in people, to appreciate personalities of many types, and to discover hidden depths of feeling in persons not blessed with easy friendship. Increase, we pray, the sensitivity with which you have endowed us. Increase it so that we may never fail to know the helpful words, the heartwarming thoughts, or the lasting comfort we can give in an hour of need.

May your love come into each heart here today. May our hands be hands through which you can work in the world. May our minds be minds through which Christ thinks, and may our hearts be hearts through which Christ loves and understands. May our lives be lives through which you can speak to all of the larger life. Amen.

Handel's Messiah

George H. Klinefelter (b. 1919), an ordained minister in the United Church of Christ, used the following as an invocation prior to the singing of Handel's *Messiah*.

God almighty, Creator of the universe, Father of our Lord Jesus Christ and our Father, you do not need our voices, for you are surrounded by an angelic choir that makes our best efforts sound like feeble echoes. Yet it pleased you to give to human beings such as George Frederick Handel and others the ability to put into music the feelings of praise and gratitude that they felt toward you and that we now find expresses our feelings as well. Continue, O God, to share with us the heavenly sounds of praise and adoration that continually surround your heavenly throne so that our humble efforts may not only be a way of expressing our faith but will also encourage and inspire others to seek for and find your message of salvation.

Use us, O God, to tell others of the Messiah, and as the message is shared once again, may it find an abiding place in our lives so that when the echoes in this hall fall silent, they shall continue to vibrate in our lives and thrill us ever again and again until we are permitted to join the heavenly hosts. In the name of the Messiah, we offer this prayer. Amen.

Heritage Sunday

Millard Osborne (b. 1932) is pastor of the East Bend Mennonite Church, Fisher, Illinois.

God of drama,
God of history,
God of heaven and earth,
We center our thoughts today on the
    great foundation stones of our heritages.
We remember, with wonder and amazement,
    the stories of your doings throughout history.
We remember, with gratitude,
    our own histories,
    the stories of our own experiences,
    and those of our parents,
    and our grandparents,
    and all our ancestors.
We are aware that here
    in our fellowship we represent a
    rich variety of heritages, and
    we celebrate that awareness.
O God, remembering our unique histories
    brings into focus several distinct responses:
    sometimes we grieve and lament the
    pain and suffering and failures
    those experiences included;
    sometimes we are bewildered when
    we try to find meaning and purpose in
    those happenings;
    and sometimes we are joyful when we
    understand how you were continually
    at work, loving and caring for
    each one, as a parent does for each child.
Through it all, we have been moved closer
    to a trust relationship with you, O Lord.

God, our heavenly Parent,
 not only are you God of the past,
 you are also God of the present
 and of the future.
 You know the end of time from its beginning.
 We express our trust in you
 by our daily commitment
 to walk in your ways,
 to live out kingdom precepts,
 to love, help, heal,
 to serve as Jesus Christ has shown us.
We desire to live out our trust in you
 as we continue to create history
 for our children and grandchildren
 by following you,
 the God of history.
To the God of Abraham, Isaac and Jacob,
 Sarah, Rebekah, Leah and Rachel,
 the God of Peter, James and John,
 Mary and Martha,
 the God of Conrad, Felix, and Menno,
 the God of our foremothers and fathers
 and our spiritual forebears,
 to you, we pray. Amen.

Anniversary of a church

Lester Hostetler (1892-1989), pastor and compiler of the *Mennonite Hymnary* (Faith and Life Press, 1940) offered this prayer on the occasion of the seventy-fifth anniversary of the Bethel College Mennonite Church, North Newton, Kansas, in November 1972. He gave permission to change the pronouns, although he always used and preferred the older language.

Almighty God, we thank you for your mercies, which are new every morning; for your loving kindnesses, which have never failed us; for the love of family and friends; for strength sufficient for our needs. We thank you for the beauty of the earth, but above all, we thank you for the Christ, whom you sent into the world so that whosoever believes on him should not perish but have everlasting life. We thank you for the record of his ministry, how he healed the sick, opened the eyes of the blind, unstopped the ears of the deaf, made the lame to walk and the dumb to speak, and raised the dead to life. We thank you for his obedience, even unto the death of the cross, and for his glorious resurrection in power. We thank you for the coming of the Holy Spirit.

We thank you, Lord, that you moved your followers in the power of the resurrection to establish the fellowship of the church in which we share, for the way in which you led your people through the centuries. We call reverently to mind the early disciples and the apostles and the martyrs of the faith.

We thank you for the pioneers of the Reformation, for their preaching of salvation by faith, their exaltation of the Bible as the Word of God, and the fidelity of their followers in time of persecution. Give us understanding hearts that we may know the precious heritage that we have in the church.

We thank you, God, for this church, for its pioneers in the seventy-five years of work, for its sacred memories of chil-

nearly 100 yrs

dren that were consecrated, of young people that were baptized, for memories of the final rites of those who have passed away, for the service it has rendered in the community and throughout the world.

We pray that you will let the sense of holiness preserve the church from false standards and from fickle change or cowardly compromise. In a time of the world's needs, give us hope. May the church keep before it the vision of the day spoken of by the ancient prophet, "They shall beat their swords into plowshares and their spears into pruning hooks and shall not learn war any more."

We thank you for Bethel College, for whom this church was first organized, for its leaders. We know that many good gifts have been bequeathed to us because of the past and the unselfish services of countless men and women. We pray your blessing to rest upon the president of the college, upon the faculty, and upon its students. Help that all may recognize you as the source of all true wisdom and love.

On this day of celebration, we also remember with gratitude many loved ones who once walked with us in blessed fellowship but have ended their earthly career to be with you. We thank you for the tender ties that bind us to the future and for the faith that dispels the shadows of earth and fills the saddest moments of life with the light of an everlasting hope. We come into your presence also confessing our sins, our unworthiness of your gifts, for we have not always loved as we ought, nor have we always been tenderhearted and forgiving of one another, as you for Christ's sake have forgiven us. We have lived in selfishness and worldly pride, and the good gifts which you have bestowed upon us we have not always devoted to your cause.

We pray that you will not deal with us after our iniquities but according to the infinite riches of your grace. We remember all those who are infirm, those who are sick, the sad, the heavy-laden, and all who mourn. Grant them the peace of those who put their trust in you.

Now let your presence inspire us, inspire our brothers and sisters to speak to us, open our minds to the truth you have for us. Grant us to know our duty as members of the church. Help us to follow the clear leading of your Spirit. In the name of Christ our Lord and Master. Amen.

As true lovers quarrel

Melvin D. Schmidt used this prayer at a meeting of the Mennonite World Conference in Wichita, Kansas, on July 30, 1978. For information about him, see the note on page 72.

For glimpses of beauty and moments of truth,
for the taste of justice and the feel of freedom,
for music that lifts our spirits sunward,
for laughter that binds loving hearts together,
for stars and dewdrops, mountains and molecules,
for all things large and small that make life livable and lovable,
Lord, we bless you; Lord, we thank you; God we love you.

And because you have loved this world so much,
Grant us now, O God,
the grace to love this world enough to quarrel with it.
To quarrel only as true lovers quarrel;
to quarrel with everything that subtracts from life,
with that magnificence and that beauty which you want to add to it.
To quarrel with superficial values:
 the glitter of nice words which conceal a disguised
 indifference,
 the sham of pious pretensions which conceal an
 unloving spirit.
To quarrel with false allegiances:
 allegiance to one race rather than the human race,

allegiance to one state rather than the state of
humankind,
allegiance to one country rather than one world,
allegiance to one denomination rather than one church,
allegiance to one city rather than the global village.
To quarrel with:
those who use bad means to try to bring about good
ends,
those who use violence to bring peace,
those who use deception to bring about justice,
those who divide people in order to unite them again
under smaller and more trivial banners.
For we know, O God, that truth can never be born of
falsehood,
and good can never be the illegitimate child of evil.
Number us now, O God, among those
who go forth from this place
not shrinking from responsibility,
but accepting it.
Make us the willing and eager inheritors
not only of the priceless legacies of the past
but also the costly challenges of the future.
Grant us, O God, yet one more grace:
to accept this broken and bleeding world
as a gift from you,
a bleeding world
for which you are still bleeding.
Take now our bodies and bleed through them.
Take our minds and think.
Take our lips and speak.
Take our hands and work.
Take our hearts and set them on fire. Amen.

Sentence prayers

Jesus said, "When you are praying, do not heap up empty phrases as the Gentiles do; for they think that they will be heard because of their many words." Matthew 6:7

God grant me the serenity to accept the things I cannot change, courage to change the things I can, and the wisdom to know the difference.
—*Reinhold Niebuhr (1892-1971)*

Lord Jesus Christ, Son of God, have mercy on me a sinner!
—*Traditional Jesus prayer of Eastern Orthodox monks*

Lord, turn my sighs into songs.
—*Robert Raines (b. 1926)*

Lord, let me not be useless.
—*John Wesley (1703-1791)*

Our families in your arms enfold
As you did keep your folk of old.
—*Pauline Krehbiel Raid (1907-1984)*

O God, make us children of quietness and heirs of peace.
—*Syrian Clementine Liturgy*

May I be to thee
What my hand is to me.
—*Source Unknown*

O Lord, help us to be masters of ourselves,
that we may be servants of others.
—*Alexander Paterson*

As you will; what you will; when you will.
—*Thomas a Kempis (1380-1471)*

Index

service 81
Shelly, Maynard 60
Shisler, Barbara Esch 7
Simons, Thomas G. 38
Sommers, Monroe 34
Sommers Rich, Elaine iii
special occasions 41-53
Sprunger, Lillian Lantz
  Rich 45, 48, 81
Stackley, Muriel
  Thiessen 40
Stevenson, Robert Louis 27
Stoltzfus, Grant M. 52
Strayer, Paul Moore 50, 67,
  73
Stutzman Kanagy, Judy 69
Sunday evening 43
Sunday worship 42, 56
Syrian Clementine
  Liturgy 90

table graces 33-40
Teresa, Mother 15
Thanksgiving 50 70
Thiessen Stackley,
  Muriel 40
Tileston Wilder, Mary 28

Toews, Aron P. 14, 22
trees 50

Ulrich, Cara 34
university 69

voluntary service 81
Voth, Carolyn Harder 32;
  John and Carolyn Harder
  31, 39

war 75
wedding 77
wedding anniversary 78
Wedel, P. J. 37
Wesley, John 39, 90
Weston, Rebecca J. 12
Whiston, Charles Francis 9
Whitehead, Grace 9
Wilder, Mary Tileston 28

Yoder, Harry 56, 62, 77
Yost, Burton G. 78; Elnore
  Rosenberger 80

Zacharias Kruger, Helen 28,
  36